FROM HELL TO HEAVEN

MY REAL LIFE TESTIMONIES AND GUIDE TO

SALVATION WITH JESUS CHRIST.

LADON PATTON

TABLE OF CONTENTS

INTRODUCTION

I always knew when I decided to seek GOD, and grow spiritually, GOD would use me for His purpose. I went through trying times in my life, but GOD allowed these trials to test me, and to share these testimonies with the world. So, I surrendered, and I sought the LORD to be better. I recognised I had to withdraw from sin, lukewarm will not get you into the Kingdom of GOD. It came on my spirit to write these testimonies as I was sharing one with someone who appears to be struggling with his faith and belief. Once I gave him some of my testimony, he said one word, which was WOW! After that conversation it was days before I heard from him again.

I knew my testimony had a spiritual effect on him, and it was that moment, I knew I had to write this guide and give these testimonies to the world. I hope this guide to salvation will reach millions, and maybe even billions, to lead them to JESUS CHRIST; and the Kingdom of GOD. Each event is factual and true. I pray you who read these incredible testimonies, believe them, and give your life to JESUS CHRIST. He who loved you enough to die for your sins, so you may have eternal life and not eternal damnation.The world we live in is becoming more sinister by the day, and according to Revelation; the end is near. Nations will rise against nations as the beast prepares to come.

Revelation 13:1 And I stood up on the sand of the sea, and saw a beast rise up out of the sea, having 7 heads and 10 horns, and upon his horns 10 crowns and upon his head the name of blasphemy.

My testimonies, though they were hard, and some even life changing, will be a blessing in someone's life. I pray the Holy Spirit is with you, to lead and guide your understanding, and your heart. GOD bless all who reads this and may it guide you to JESUS CHRIST! In JESUS NAME! AMEN! When we live for JESUS CHRIST and accept him as our SAVIOR, he nourishes and protects us just like we do our children. JESUS, YESHUA, THE MESSIAH gave his life for you. Will you give your life for him? I have always said, humans are not capable of loving the way JESUS loves. We surely don't deserve his love, yet he loves us mercifully and unconditionally.

TESTIMONY #1

HOME ALONE

1 Thessolonians 5:17

Pray without ceasing

I waved goodbye, as my grandfather and my grandmother drove away, en route to the grocery store. But at 7 years of age, I was wondering why did they pack suitcases, and take them? Oh well, *I just can't wait until they return because I'm starving,* I thought. At 7 years old they raised me as one of their children even though My grandfather was the step-father. My grandmother was a single parent and didn't have any help from either of the three fathers who fathered her six children. I truly admire my grandfather for taking on such a huge responsibility, or at least trying to. Out of the six kids my grandmother had, there were only 2 at home, plus me. They raised me as their own when my mother left. I was only 3 months old, and she was 15 years old. My mother told me when I became an adult, that my grandfather tried to have inappropriate relations with her and when she told my grandmother; she told her she was a liar and refused to believe her. So my mother left, she didn't return until I was almost 6 years old, and even then, she wasn't ready to be a mother. Now previous to this my grandmother told me she was my mother, and my grandfather was my father, so I presumed this to be true. The day my grandmother and grandfather left me and my 2 uncles, who were age 13 and age 16, they left in the early morning and it was now almost nightfall. My stomach felt like it was touching my back. My uncles sat with a blank stare before we decided to rummage through the kitchen looking for anything to eat. We had bread and water, then we went to sleep just to forget about being hungry, if for nothing else. At sunrise, we woke up, still hungry from the previous day. We went to check my grandparents' room, but still no sign of them, and we were even hungrier than the day before! And so was King, King was my 16-year-old uncle Edward's Doberman Pinscher, my uncle Edward stood to his feet angrily as he said.

"I can't take this anymore," and he hit the streets begging, and stealing food, which would become a regular routine for him. My uncle and I—who was only 13 years old—went to school, the only place we could eat, besides the bits of food uncle Edward came home with. Well, about a week later my aunt drove from Oklahoma to Kansas where we stayed, to pick up her daughter. My grandparents (who we later found out moved to Oklahoma) instructed my aunt Vette to pick up my uncle Allan and bring him back to Oklahoma. I was sad, my buddy was leaving me. Uncle Allan and I were very close, and Edward only came home every 2 to 3 days. So it was just me and King. The next day after school, I came home and heard laughter and talking coming from my grandparent's bedroom, I thought to myself *yay they are back*, I ran to the bedroom, and it was my mother; whom I had only seen once prior to this. Accompanied by a man," she looked up to see me. Her eyes were glaring at mines as she was laying in this man's arms. My mother introduced me to this man as her little sister as she smiled at me and said.

"I got you some food and clothes."

I looked at the second-hand clothes sprawled out on the bed, and I was grateful for what she had given me. But I wanted the food ASAP! For a minute, I felt happy again. She warmed a can of Spaghettios, and fed me, then she was preparing to leave with her male companion despite my pleas not to leave.

"I'll be back, I promise."

She turned to me, and said, but somehow I knew she would not come back. Actually, nobody came for quite some time. It was just me, and King; and the hungrier he got, the more afraid I became. In the coming days, I went to school to eat if nothing else. I did not know a lot about GOD yet, but I always felt a pleasant presence there with me. To this day, I don't know how long I was alone, but it seemed like forever. I survived on the food from school, but on the weekends I was on my own. I went to a church close to my house for food.

I do not know how I knew to go there, but I did. I told them I was hungry, and they fed me. I did not tell anyone I was alone, but they knew something was not right. I would walk around the neighborhood during the day. At night I made certain to return to the house with no food and no running water. I didn't know how to lock the front door, but I knew how to shut it. So, I would shut the front door, put King in the bedroom with me and lock the bedroom door. The one emotion I did not have was fear, perhaps my focus on food eliminated the fear, but I NEVER felt ALONE! Tonight I did my usual routine, I shut the front door, went into the bedroom and shut and locked that door, with only me and King in the bedroom. Something was different about this night, the dog was different, very different. I climbed into the bed as King stood on his hind legs at the end of the bed, staring at me. I looked at him and yelled out.

"Sit, King, sit!"

But he just kept staring, and didn't move, I climbed under the covers, and covered my head, then I heard a growl come from him like never before. I took the covers off of my head only to see King's demonic transformation, his eyes glowed red like a dog in a horror movie. I glanced to my left at the closet door thinking to myself, *if I can get in that closet I can lock myself in there where he can't get me.* As I was thinking about a getaway, King became more aggressive, I shivered in fear. For the 1st time since this entire ordeal started, I feared. I screamed for help, as what appeared to be a demon dog leaped through the air to charge at me when the unbelievable and supernatural happened! My small body was lifted through the air and within 2 seconds this invisible, powerful force placed me within the closet, and slammed the door. I heard the dog fighting with this invisible force I could not see. As I sat in the dark closet, I could hear the sounds of vicious fighting, and then I did not hear the dog anymore. I then tried to open the closet, which had no lock on it, but yet it remained locked. I knew it was an angel, the same angel that had been with me, which was the very reason I never felt alone. The closet door never opened until morning, Who knows what else GOD protected me from that night. So, I've known since I was a small child how powerful the LORD is. JESUS is so amazing. People look for scientific proof to prove JESUS exists. There is no science in the supernatural power of GOD! His power is so great, no man or science project can come near his power. However, many theologians, archaeologists, and even missionaries have found proof of biblical events.

Within a day or so the neighbors realized I was alone and took me in, they somehow reached my grandmother who drove back to Kansas to get me. I believe that was the work of GOD himself. My mother only returned once with a chicken leg and $2. I later found out my grandmother left my mother money for food, and to pay the bills at the house; and she was to stay there with me. My grandmother did not know I was alone, and she was not happy about it. I eventually forgave my mother. When I became an adult, I was her caretaker when she was dying of cancer, and then I buried her. She put men before me my whole life, but not one of them was around when she was sick. You see, you never know how GOD will act in your life or how he will use you. But what we know is He loves us and hates sin. Yes, GOD loved us enough to give his only begotten son.

John 3:16 For GOD so loved the world, that he gave his only begotten son, that whosoever believeth in him should not perish, but have everlasting life.

2) Timothy 3:2-7 For men shall be lovers of their own selves, covetous, boasters, proud, blasphemers, disobedient to parents, unthankful, unholy. 3) Without natural affection, trucebreakers, false accusers, incontinent, fierce, despisers of those that are good.

4) Traitors, heady, high minded, lovers of pleasures more than lovers of GOD; 5) Having a form of Godliness but denying the power thereof: from such turn away

6) For of this sort are they which creep into houses, and lead captive silly women laden with sins, led away with divers lust, 7 always learning and never able to come to the knowledge of the truth

The scripture clearly gives a long list of what NOT to do, as well as what to do. The LORD left us specific instructions until his return. If you look at the world today and the list in Timothy, you will notice everything on the list is exactly

what we see in the world around us today. The deception of the enemy has made it look right, while knowing in the eyes of the LORD JESUS it's wrong. GOD gave us free will. It's either a yes or a no, but there is no middle. You can't have your cake and eat it too. Being a Christian is a beautiful experience. Once I truly became saved GOD gave me the gift of the HOLY SPIRIT, and it's the most amazing experience I've ever had. When you really become saved and I don't mean "lukewarm" I mean saved. You actually have the desire to do good and avoid sin. You have the desire to want to help others get to where you are and spread the message. I know people think it's no fun being a Christian, but it actually is. You don't have to be buried in sin to have fun. You just have to do as the LORD asks of you, which comes naturally, unless you love your sin more than you do GOD. I'd much rather be a saint than a sinner.

TESTIMONY #2

TERRIBLE TWISTER

Nahum 1:3 The LORD is slow to anger, and great in power, and will not at all acquit the wicked: the LORD has his way in the whirlwind and in the storm, and the clouds are dust of his feet.

It was May 3rd, 1999, a bright sunny day with a 30% chance of rain in the forecast. I'm now 29 yrs old with 2 sons, one was 5 and one was almost 10. My 10 year old was at school and my 5 year old was at a relative's house. I had just had lunch with my friend. After lunch I went to visit some more friends of mine, Jackie and Cletus, a married couple. As we were visiting, we took notice of the weather on the news. It seemed to be really serious. The news forecaster Gary England, was seemingly nervous as he reported combining tornados in our vicinity. It was strange how all these little tornados kept attaching to the big one, which would soon go on to make one of the largest, most ferocious tornados in American history. There hasn't been another tornado this deadly since then. The Richter scales went to a F5 this monster classified as an F6, and it was headed straight for us.

I looked at the clock and realized I had to rush and get my son from school. When I got to my son's school and picked him up, he knew something was wrong, So he looked at me and said,

"What's wrong mama?"

I said, "it's awful weather coming soon, we gotta get home!"

He said, "Okay mama."

So I went home and turned the TV on to check the weather. At that moment, my greatest fear was facing me. This monster of a tornado has grown 2 ½ miles wide with over 250mph winds on the ground wreaking havoc, and there were still small tornadoes combining with it to get bigger! Before it was finished it had grown over 3 miles wide, with over 350mph winds, and it was getting closer and closer to us.

I looked at my son and said, "we have to get your brother."

My baby said. "Mama, I'm scared."

And I told him, "don't be afraid we will pray, come on let's go we have got to get to your baby brother."

We got in the car and the sky was eerie and dark, and the strangest feeling came over me, it was like a hurry you're running out of time, feeling, What I didn't realize was how close this monster tornado actually was. As I merged onto the highway, I noticed that the rain was heavier, cars were parking under the bridge overpasses, and EVERYBODY was speeding, even the police were speeding. That's when I knew it was serious. So, I looked in my rearview mirror as I sped up, and all I saw was darkness and debris flying around in the air.

I said, "OH MY GOD! The tornado is right behind me."

I looked at my baby boy and said.

"Pray baby mama is about to floor it."

I drove my Honda Prelude to the maximum speed, and made it to my exit in maybe 5min, and I was about 5 miles away. As I exited off the highway, I was a nervous wreck, but I knew I had to get us to safety. I talked to GOD the entire time, asking for his help and protection, but as I was talking to GOD, I was afraid. In my mind it was a terrifying situation, not to mention this beast of a tornado was traveling the same path I was. I made it to my cousin's house; we rushed through the door and I picked my 5 year old up, hugged and kissed him as I grabbed my other son's hand. I watched a few minutes of the weather forecast; I turned to look at my cousin and told her.

"This thing is heading straight for us and we need to seek shelter."

So we all gathered up and drove to the nearest school. I called my mom and told them to meet us at the school. When we arrived at the school my mom was already pulling in. We all parked in the elementary school's parking lot and got out. There were others pulling in to seek shelter. When we got out of the car there was an overpowering gas odor in the air from busted gas lines, then the tornado sirens sounded off. I was terrified because that means the tornado is close, FEAR had overcome me. My mom looked at me and said.

"You all don't have FAITH, you gotta have FAITH!"

As the tornado got closer, the school officials moved everyone inside, My fear was growing, but what my mom said stuck with me, I was not having FAITH! Once we all got in the building, they guided us down a ramp. It wasn't completely underground, but it was the best we had, the tornado was less than a mile away. We all took a seat wherever we could and someone suggested that we pray. My mom looked at me and the terror on my face and said, "Have FAITH."

As the tornado was getting closer, we were all praying hard. There was a 4 way intersection, 2 blocks away from the school, the tornado got to that intersection and actually stopped at the stop sign; it was said that the tornado just sat at the stop sign for a few minutes. I believe that was when we were praying; the tornado eventually went east turning right, because had it kept straight it would have been a direct hit on the school we were in. There was a lot of prayer that day and GOD heard them, but he only answers the prayer with faith. GOD sent the tornado away from us that day, and I learned a valuable lesson, FAITH OVER FEAR!!

Psalms 23:4 Yea, though I walk through the valley of the shadow of death I will fear no evil: for thou art with me, thy rod and thy staff they comfort me.

Deuteronomy 31:6 Be strong and of a good courage, fear not, nor be afraid of them, for the LORD thy GOD he it is that doth go with thee: he will not fail thee, nor forsake thee.

Psalms 27:1-5 The LORD is my light and my salvation; whom shall I fear? The LORD is the strength of my life; of whom shall I be afraid? 2 When the wicked, even mine enemies and my foes, came upon me to eat up my flesh, they stumbled and fell. 3 Though a host should encamp against me, my heart shall not fear; though war shall arise against me, in this will I be confident. 4 One thing have I desired of the LORD, that will I seek after; that I may dwell in the house of the LORD all the days of my life, to behold the beauty of the LORD, and to inquire in his temple. 5 For in the time of trouble, shall hide me in his pavilion; in the secret of his tabernacle shall he hide me; he shall set me upon a rock.

Isaiah 41:10 "So do not fear, for I am with you; do not be dismayed, for I am your GOD. I will strengthen you and help you; I will uphold you with my righteous right hand."

Phillippians 4:6-7 "Do not be anxious about anything, but in every situation, by prayer and petition, with thanksgiving, present your requests to GOD. And the peace of GOD, which transcends all understanding will guard your hearts and your minds in CHRIST

There are people who love their sin so much, that they have denounced the Holy Bible. They look for any reason to condemn GOD's word or they even try to manipulate the words in the Holy Bible. They love their sin so much they will come to any conclusion to stay in it. The Holy Bible is the,"*Basic Instruction before leaving earth.*" GOD's Prophecies have and will come to pass. The scripture says, "no man knows the day or the hour," If JESUS comes right now. Are you ready? Can you say you will go with the LORD if he comes right now? If your answer is "no" you should do some soul searching and make the most important decision of your life. GOD gave us free will to choose to worship and love him. I don't know about you but I choose the beauty of heaven, and more importantly, the love and protection of JESUS CHRIST.

Isaiah 41;10 So do not fear, for I am with you; do not be dismayed, for I am your GOD. I will strengthen you and help you; I will uphold you with my righteous right hand.

Deuteronomy 31:8 The LORD himself goes before you and will be with you; he will never leave you nor forsake you, fear not, neither be dismayed

The love of GOD is beautiful, merciful, loving, nourishing, and I can go on and on. He has protected me my entire life. JESUS loves us all, and he showed it that day on the Cross.

James 1:17 Every good and perfect gift is from above, coming down from the Father of the heavenly lights, who does not change like shifting shadows.

TESTIMONY #3

ANGEL WARNINGS

Psalms 34:7 The Angel of the LORD encamps round about them that fear him and rescues them.

I used to be a gambler; it seemed as if I was having luck at the bingo hall, so I wanted to go to the casino to try my luck. I went home after the bingo hall closed and had a bite to eat and tried to talk myself out of going to the casino. An overwhelming desire came over me to go. So I started trying to find someone to go with me, but I was unsuccessful. As I was sitting thinking of who could go, I heard this voice in my right ear saying *no don't go!* I thought to myself, *am I going crazy? What was that? So,* I shook it off as I debated with myself and decided to go, but that voice in my ear was coming frequently. *Don't go! It* said over and over. Then I felt the feeling of a very strong presence, but I still headed for the door. The closer I got to the door I had the worse feeling, but I still went out the door and as I stepped off of the porch to walk toward the sidewalk, I heard the voice getting louder in my right ear.

"DON'T GO!"

Yet I kept walking, and suddenly I saw an almost translucent sort of white figure to the right of me. It yelled in my ear with a supernatural force as I felt hot air on the right side of my face.

"DON'T GO!"

My hair blew as the supernatural force spoke! Terrified, I turned and ran back in the house, yelling.

"OKAY! OKAY! I'm not going!"

I shouted as I shut and locked the door. I knew then it was an angel warning me, and I thank GOD the angel manifested itself because I was not listening. I don't know what awaited me on that late night trip to the casino, but whatever it was, GOD himself didn't want me to meet that fate. Do you hear the voices of warning sometimes? If you do, believe that it's GOD'S angels warning you, the Angel won't always manifest itself.

Proverbs 3:2 And the Angel of the LORD appeared unto him in a flame of fire out of the midst of a bush; and he looked and behold the bush was not consumed.

Angels are so beautiful and powerful. GOD sends them to protect, to send messages and warnings, and even to fight our battles. You see, people live in the flesh more than they do the spirit. Living in the flesh brings worldly ways and worldly thoughts. Living in the spirit is living in the ways of GOD. No one shall enter the Kingdom of Heaven living in the flesh. You have to learn to live in the spiritual and the natural on a daily basis. There are Angels helping you even with the smaller things in life, that big job interview, the approval for a house, your spouse, and many other things. Angels even whisper in your ear to wake you up in the time of danger. I'm sure plenty of you have experienced that, but we always said something woke me up. That something is GOD'S Angels. Once you grow spiritually with JESUS CHRIST, you will recognize when you are having a supernatural experience. GOD speaks to all of us, but some of us are so buried in sin we can't hear Him.

You see many will follow the beast, even worship him, the same beast that will drag them to hell with him. This is what the Bible says will happen to you if you worship the beast.

Revelation 14:9-10   9 And the third angel followed them saying with a loud voice, If any man shall worship the beast and his image , and receive his mark in his forehead or in his hand 10 the same shall drink the wrath of GOD which is poured out without mixture into the cup of his indignation; and will be tormented with fire and brimstone in the presence of the Holy Angels and in the presence of the lambs.

The plagues we are experiencing were prophesied in Revelation, described as GOD's wrath. Now is a time where we must all ask ourselves do we want to be in GOD'S good graces or will you be one of the ones to incur GOD'S HOLY WRATH?

Revelations 15:1   And I saw another sign in Heaven, great and marvelous, seven angels having the seven lost plagues; for in them is filled up the wrath of GOD.

The end is near. Are you ready? Do you believe in JESUS CHRIST and accept him as your personal savior? If you haven't now is the time to accept Him. If you're a non-believer now is the time to believe.

John 20:31 "but these have been written so that you may believe that JESUS is the CHRIST, the Son of GOD life, and that believing you may have in his name.

Act 16:31 They said, "believe in the LORD JESUS and you will be saved, you and   your household.

John 6:47 Truly, truly I say to you, he who believes has eternal life.

Are you ready to give your life to JESUS CHRIST? If so, repeat what's below.

I _____ confess and repent of my sins, those that are known, unknown, and the sins and iniquities of my heart. I ask that JESUS CHRIST comes into my heart as I accept you JESUS as my LORD and PERSONAL SAVIOR. I believe in you LORD JESUS. I love you LORD JESUS, and I accept you JESUS CHRIST in my life and I am ready to live my life for you LORD JESUS. In JESUS' name I pray. AMEN

Now live your life for CHRIST, turn away from sin, and let him guide you. Yet if you sin, quickly repent and do good. Study your HOLY BIBLE with your peers. Congratulations, you just chose Heaven instead of hell.

Remember there are times you will be tested GOD can allow certain events to happen in your life to test your faith, please don't take it personally, As you can see, I have been tested throughout this whole book. GOD'S most faithful servant in the Bible, Job was tested beyond limits. Job had everything, and Satan attacked him in unimaginable ways, yet Job remained faithful to GOD. GOD blessed Job with everything he had and more for remaining faithful. GOD'S love always wins.

IMPORTANT BIBLE SCRIPTURES

John 3:16 *For God so loved the world he gave his only Son, that whosoever believeth in him should not perish but have eternal life.*

Romans 10: 9-10 *If you declare with your mouth "JESUS IS LORD", and believe in your heart that GOD raised him from the dead, you will be saved. 10 For it is with your heart that you believe and are justified, and it is with your mouth that you profess your faith and be saved. Mark 16:16*

Whoever believes and is baptized will be saved, but whoever does not believe will be condemned.

Romans 10:13 *For everyone who calls on the name of the LORD will be saved.*

Matthew 10:22 *You will be hated by everyone because of me,but the one who stands firm to the end will be saved.*

AFTERWORD I

I trust JESUS CHRIST will guide and bless you on your journey to salvation.

There will be many deceivers who try to lure you away from JESUS CHRIST with their false teachings, made-up religions,

and sinful spirits. But remember, the enemy is working overtime to steal your soul. Walk with JESUS, and obey his commandments, and if you sin quickly repent, for no man knows his last day, hour, or minute. Lead other lost souls to JESUS CHRIST. And beware of this quote.

"The BIBLE is not real and has been changed."

Do not fall for it. It's the biggest trick of the enemy. If you don't believe the Bible, then you don't believe in all the very important teachings of the Bible. Such as the death and the resurrection of JESUS CHRIST, and if you don't believe that, then you do not make it to HEAVEN. I will leave you with what GOD said about those who try to alter or change the BIBLE.

Revelation 22:18-21   18 For I testify unto every man that heareth the words of the prophecy of this book, If any man shall add unto these things, GOD shall add unto him the plagues that are written in this book. 19 And if any man shall take away from the words of this prophecy, GOD shall take away his part out of the book of life, and out of

the Holy City, and from the things which are written in this book. 20 He which testifieth

these things saith, surely I come quickly. Even so, come, LORD JESUS. 21 The grace of our LORD JESUS CHRIST be with you all. Amen

I wrote this book with love to help lead people to eternal life with JESUS CHRIST.

I hope and pray it reached the hearts of many. Will you choose eternal life? Or eternal damnation? It's your choice. GOD gave you free will.

--L. Patton Christian Author

TESTIMONY #4

MIRACLE BABY

Psalms 139; 1 13-14 13 For thou hast possessed my reins: thou hast covered me in my mother's womb. 14 I will praise thee; for I am fearfully and wonderfully made; marvellous are thy works: and that my soul knoweth right well.

It's 2003 and I've just been told I was pregnant again, my last baby isn't even one yet I thought, and this will be baby number four. I lived with my two sons and my daughter, J who was thirteen years of age, Roy who was eight years of age, and Rayen was nine months old. Ricky, my boyfriend, and the father of my youngest child, lived with us too. I worked the whole time I was pregnant with Rayen until I had her. I was a sterile tech in the surgery department at a local hospital. I was not happy about the pregnancy; I am very sick when I am pregnant and I hadn't fully recovered from my last pregnancy, but the main issue was Ricky and I was on rocky ground. He was a serial cheater and had to grow up. His idea of life was partying at the club, women, and his friends. He wasn't ready for family life, while I worked the night shift, he had another woman on the side. I suspected such, but I wasn't sure, so one night I got ahold of Ricky's phone and listened to his voicemail messages when I heard a woman's voice saying.

"Baby, where are you, I'm sitting here waiting on you?"

Ricky told me he was going to a nightclub, but he was really going to this woman's house. I stormed into the house to confront him. We had a huge argument, and I put him out. Ricky packed a few of his belongings and went straight to the woman we were arguing about. I felt betrayed, alone, and pregnant. *What will I do now? I* asked myself. The next day I woke up still hurting about what happened. I did some heavy thinking this day and decided I wanted to have an abortion, but GOD had another plan. I was outside smoking a cigarette, thinking how and when I would get an abortion, when suddenly I heard a voice that said.

"You better not go get an abortion for if you do you will not make it off the abortion table!"

Now this voice was stern and powerful, I knew it was the voice of GOD and I feared! The thought of an abortion immediately left my mind. I also reminded myself 6 months prior to this, my mother came to me and said,

"GOD told me you will get pregnant again, and will be a girl."

And now here I am, pregnant just as she testified the LORD told her.

I kept my baby, and reconciled with Ricky for the sake of our children, so I thought. At six and a half months I was rushed to the hospital with contractions. They tried to give me medicine to keep the baby in my womb, but to no avail; my water broke, and I was rushed into emergency surgery for a cesarean because she was coming out breech (feet first). I had her at 29 weeks and was terrified for my baby. The doctor who delivered her was excellent, built like a professional athlete, he was big and stout; he held my baby in one of his huge hands, her head was at his fingertips, and her feet were at the palm of his hands. She weighed one and a half pounds. I couldn't even hold her; she had to be rushed to the neonatal intensive care unit. I had her on Mother's Day, yet I was devastated and not feeling so well myself. They took me upstairs to a room and got me settled in, this was the beginning of a long hard journey.

It was 2 days before I saw my daughter again once I was strong enough to walk down to the NICU. I walked in and seeing this small body in an incubator, she was hooked up to all kinds of tubing and monitors. She had IV's all over her and I became sad and scared. The doctors came and talked to me and told me,

"Look, we know it looks bad, but your daughter will be fine. It will take a while and extensive treatments, but we believe she will be fine."

Somehow I knew she would be fine. It looked scary, but when GOD has a plan, nothing is impossible. I named her Heaven because she was a blessing from GOD and she was truly from Heaven. The nurses in the NICU were very comforting. The doctor explained my baby's treatments and condition, he said that due to Heaven's prematurity, her heart didn't fully develop, and that when she got a little older, it would have to be surgically corrected. This was hard for me, all parents want their children to be healthy, so something like this was life changing. Two months passed before I knew it. I was at the hospital everyday visiting my baby. I had to feed, bathe, and change her each day I went to see her, it was part of the bonding process. My daughter was very sick, but she was a real fighter. She was growing by the day and getting stronger. I had 3 other kids at home to take care of, so I had a very heavy plate. Remember GOD won't put more on you than you can stand. Ricky was there for the hospital visits, but he still had some growing up to do. I knew he would grow up one day, but for now I knew I had to step up to be there for baby Heaven.

It was getting close to the time to bring baby Heaven home. I had to take classes to learn how to care for a special needs baby and prepare our home with the proper medical equipment. Also find a nurse to come in and assist with her care.

The day came to bring baby Heaven home, we were all so excited, but I was both excited and scared. Heaven was on a heart monitor and oxygen. Her first night home she had a grand mal seizure and ended up right back in the hospital for two weeks. I felt in my heart that it was too soon for her to come home and I was right. After two more weeks in the hospital and lots of treatment, Heaven was ready to come home, and we were so thrilled to have her home. Ricky was the only one working now, I had to devote myself full time to the care of Heaven, it was hard financially, but GOD always made a way.

So I had to figure out how to give this special care and attention to my baby and still give my other children the attention they needed, I figured it out. I wanted to be the best mom I could be, and I strived to be just that. Heaven was developing and gaining weight. She was thriving and fighting. Her strength amazed me. We had frequent trips to the cardiologist, her heart condition needed close monitoring. The doctor put her on seizure medicine, but miraculously she never had another seizure. Now I may not have been a devout Christian, but I always knew GOD, and I always believed JESUS was my LORD and SAVIOR!

I reached out to a very powerful, anointed female minister who held prayer meetings for me and my family. Her testimony of how she came to GOD is amazing. Sister Pauline was her name, a mild, meek woman whose faith was unmoving. She told us she was suffering from uterine cancer and while she was in the last stages on her deathbed in the hospital, the doctors had already called her family and gave her twelve to twenty-four hours to live and that they should make funeral arrangements. But as she laid there she cried out to GOD and asked Him to save her. She promised Him she would do His work if He will only allow her to live. Well, she gave her testimony 15 years later, so as you can see GOD granted her wish. Her 24hrs to live turned into years. GOD can do it. He did not perform His work. She could see what we couldn't and blessed a holy gift of sight and vision. GOD spoke to her, and she clearly heard Him. Her prayers rang powerfully, and full of faith. I knew I wanted her prayers of healing over my baby girl Heaven. I took the time and called Sister Pauline asking her to come and pray over baby Heaven, for healing. Sister Pauline agreed, and she came within a week, but this time she wasn't alone. She brought some extra Holy power with her; she brought her brother, who was also a powerful Pastor by his own right, and another woman friend of hers, who was filled with the spirit of GOD. Magnificently, they joined hands while standing over my daughter and said a prayer so powerful. It filled the entire room with the Holy Spirit and brought me to tears. I truly felt the magnitude of the powerful prayer and the faith of the powerful three. When they finished praying, they left like Angels who just completed their task for JESUS. I bid my farewell to the mighty three prayer warriors, and I waited on the LORD for the healing of my daughter. The last time we went to the Cardiologist was two weeks prior to the mighty prayer, and we had to return in two weeks. The doctors were waiting on her to gain weight so they could do the heart surgery. Heaven's heart didn't fully develop due to her premature birth, and she had veins on the outside of her heart that belonged inside of her heart. A few days before Heaven's next appointment, Minister Pauline called me and she said

"LaDon,"

And I said, *"yes, ma'am?"*

And she said. "GOD told me to tell you baby Heaven's heart is healed."

I started crying as she gave all the glory to GOD! She would always say don't give me any glory, give all the glory to GOD! I thought about that phone call every day until the heart doctors appointment, all we needed now was confirmation. As Heaven and I arrived at the doctor's appointment, they took her back for normal routine testing. The test checks for any development with her heart. Up until this day, there were no changes with her heart. I patiently waited for them to bring her back from getting her test run and for the doctor to come in and give her test results. First the nurses brought baby Heaven back, and it elated me, because I knew the doctor would come in with good news. The Doctor comes in. I'm smiling away as she looks at me with a confused look on her face, then she looks at me and says,

"What are you smiling about?"

And I said, "I believe you have good news for me?"

And she looked at me in surprise and said, "yes, I have good news for you, how did you know?"

I said, "tell me the good news first and I will tell you how I knew afterwards."

So she looked at me and said, "baby Heaven's heart has healed, there's absolutely nothing wrong with her heart anymore." I was filled with joy!

"THANK YOU JESUS."

I cried out. I looked at the doctor and said, "Doc, do you believe in GOD?"

She tilted her head to the side and shrugged her shoulder, as if to say somewhat. I told her if you don't believe you should, because you just witnessed a real life miracle from GOD. I had three very powerful prayer warriors who came to my house and prayed over Heaven for healing and now here we are, we are witnessing GOD'S miracle. The Doctor's mouth dropped to the ground, with a big wow! Now I had a feeling Heaven's miracle changed the doctor's life, which makes this story that much more beautiful. I got in the car and cried with tears of joy as I kissed baby Heaven. Today Heaven is 16 years old in excellent health. GOD is REAL my brothers and sisters in CHRIST, he always has the last say.

Luke 18:27 JESUS replied, what is impossible with man is possible with GOD.

Matthew 17:20 He replied, "because you have so little faith, truly I tell you if you have faith small as a mustard seed , you can say to this mountain, move from here to there and it will move. Nothing will be impossible for you

Acts 19: 11-12 11 God did extraordinary miracles through paul. 12 so that even handkerchiefs and aprons that had touched him were taken to the sick, and their illnesses were cured and the evil spirits left them.

Prayer is the most powerful weapon it is, the power of prayer has been proven. JESUS said all you need is a mustard seed of faith and watch for your miracle. I am a witness to this. Thank you, JESUS! However, prepare yourself for when GOD'S answer is no. Sometimes His answer is no for many different reasons, just trust in him he will not lead you wrong, and remember Earth is the temporary resting place. Your true Kingdom is Heaven. GOD is faithful and just, and sometimes He protects us from ourselves. Pray without ceasing, and put on the full armour of GOD, the breastplate of righteousness, and the helmet of salvation, then go to battle in a powerful prayer. It's more effective than any man-made weapon. GOD'S children are the most powerful soldiers on the planet, because we understand the power of the spiritual world. We fight in the spirit and we appear in the flesh. For this reason we are under constant attack by the enemy. JESUS gave us authority in His mighty name to fight evil spirits and principalities of darkness. It's the enemy's mission to destroy as many of GOD'S children as he can, he's out to seek, kill, and destroy. GOD made us in his likeness, and for that reason the adversary hates us. Just look at the events taking place in the world today. The Coronavirus, one of many plagues of which the book of Revelation speaks of. Earthquakes and famines, nations rising against nations, wars and rumors of wars, hate is on a rise with racism, murder and malice, children dishonoring their parents, evil and wicked people in high places, it's all in Revelation. This is the time to study and prepare with the information GOD gave us in the Holy Bible. Deception is all around you. Do not be deceived. The Holy Bible is not just a book, it's a prophecy as well. You will see this in my breakdown of Daniel's 70 week prophecy at the end of my book. There are those skeptics who question Daniel's book in the Bible. Daniel wrote his own book and there were times he referred to himself as the third party in the book, which skeptics believe contradicts the book. Most ancient writers wrote in the third party even when speaking of themselves. Daniel was a beloved prophet of GOD who pleased GOD when he denied the royal meat and wine with the claim he didn't want to defile his body. For ten days he only took water and vegetables which pleased our LORD and he was blessed with many talents.

Daniel 1:16-17   16 Thus Mel'-zar took away the portion of their meat, and the wine that they should drink; and gave them vegetables.   17 As for these four children, GOD gave them knowledge and skill in all learning and wisdom: and Daniel had understanding in all visions and dreams. Daniel had some of the most amazing prophecies in the Holy Bible including the prophecy of the MESSIAH'S coming which you will see in Daniel's 70 week prophecy I break down in the back of this book. It shows the first coming of the MESSIAH in the Old Testament which alludes to the idea of JESUS the MESSIAH only being traced to the New Testament. Daniel prophesied many events in Revelation hundreds of years before the book of Revelation was written. The Bible really gives each event that will happen in the world, and most of it has already happened and most people don't realize it. I know many can't understand the Bible, but you have to pray for understanding. Also remember you have to STUDY the Bible, use the parallel passages it really helps. Daniel was one of GOD'S most anointed prophets. GOD showed him so many visions of what was to come. Daniel was given a night vision in chapter 7 about the Anti-Christ, which years later was written in the book of Revelation. *Daniel 7;7-8   7 After this I saw in the night visions, and behold a fourth beast, dreadful and terrible, and strong exceedingly; and it had great iron teeth: it devoured and brake in pieces, and stamped the residue with the feet of it: and it was diverse from all the beasts that were before it;* and it had ten horns. 8 I considered the horns, and, behold, there came up among them another little horn, before whom there were three of the first horns plucked up by the roots: and, behold, in this horn were eyes like the eyes of a man, and a mouth speaking great things. Please read the Daniel prophecy of CHRIST and the Anti-Christ on pg 85.

TESTIMONY #5
SAVED BY GOD'S GRACE

Ephesians 2: 8-9   8 For by grace are ye saved through faith; and that not of yourselves; it is the gift of GOD. 9 Not of works, lest any man should boast.

It was a beautiful sunny spring day, Easter Sunday to be exact. My two daughters and I were up early this morning preparing for church. I had just recently moved back to Oklahoma from Las Vegas to help my elderly grandparents, so my daughters and I were staying with them temporarily.   My grandmother is an argumentative person, she's grumpy and loves confusion at times, but we gotta love her. On this particular morning, as we were on our way to church she tried to start one of her usual quarrels. "I said *oh no, I'm on my way to church, and I will not indulge in arguing with you love.*"

So me and the girls' left, heading to church. It was a peaceful ride on the way as we were talking, laughing, and listening to gospel music. I drove up on a four-way intersection and prepared to stop but my light turned green so I proceeded to go through the intersection. I was almost through the intersection when BOOM! BAM! BOOM! A big black truck ran a red light and hit us repeatedly. After the first hit, I remember hearing my daughters' screams over and over, they were screaming "mama" and I said.

"OH my GOD."

It was the worst feeling not being able to help my children. As a parent, we want to be their protector at all times, but on this day GOD reminded me who our protector is, and that's GOD Himself. After the second hit, everything started going in slow motion, like a scene out of the Matrix movie, and BOOM! The third hit was of greater impact, the slow motion got slower and my daughters' screams became further and further away. Then out of nowhere there was a huge white image like a large blinding bright light came through the car and across my face as I looked in awe. But it left just as quickly as it came. I knew it was an Angel from heaven. After the Angel was gone, all the slow motion stopped, the car stopped spinning and got hit. I know that Holy Angel that came in the car and manifested itself saved our lives, and I am so grateful to the LORD for sending His beautiful Angel to save our lives. One thing is for sure, we were saved by GOD'S grace and mercy. A few days after the wreck, I watched the news. I saw where a woman and her daughter got hit by a man who ran a red light the same way we got hit. It killed her and her young daughter. May GOD bless and have their souls, but I felt that was GOD'S confirmation to me that He sent the Angel to save us. GOD always gives confirmation. I know my LORD JESUS has a purpose for me, and I'm willing and waiting to do whatever He wants, for I am His servant as we all are. I am GOD'S servant and very blessed to be in GOD'S beautiful

GRACE.

Matthew 6: 9-13   9   After this manner therefore pray ye: Our Father which art in heaven, Hallowed be thy name.   10   Thy kingdom come, thy will be done on earth, as it is in heaven.   11 Give us this day our daily bread.   12   And forgive us our debts as we forgive our debtors.   13   And lead us not into temptation, but deliver us from evil: for thine is the Kingdom, and the power, and the glory, for ever. Amen

Romans 10: 9-10   9   That if thou shalt confess with thy mouth the LORD JESUS, and shalt believe in thine heart that GOD hath raised him from the dead, thou shalt be saved.   10   For with the heart man believeth unto righteousness; and with the mouth confession is made unto salvation.

Acts 16:30-31 30 And brought them out, and said, "Sirs, what must I do to be saved? 31 And they said, "Believe in the LORD JESUS CHRIST, and thou shall be saved, and thy house.

All we need to do is accept JESUS as our savior, confess our sins, and have faith. GOD will bless, protect, lead, guide, and love us. We also have to be aware of false prophets and false teachings. There will come a time when the children of GOD will have to fight in a battle of doing right or wrong. The world will make the rights look wrong and the wrongs look right. Leaving the LORD'S people to be brave and fight for GOD'S truth, and the exposure of the adversary and the false prophets preaching false doctrines and misleading GOD's people. As believers in CHRIST we must be strong, bold and willing to withstand the criticism of the evildoers. The way to do that is to put on the full armour of GOD! Remember

do not be lukewarm, many Christians will perish for being lukewarm. There are those that think because they believe in CHRIST they will inherit the Kingdom, but you have to walk in his way as well, as I have explained many times throughout the book. See here what GOD says about lukewarm.

Revelation 3:16 So then because thou art lukewarm, and neither cold nor hot, I will spue thee out of my mouth.

GOD said, you should either be hot or cold, there is no in between. Most people are lukewarm because they love their sin and choose not to turn away from it. So many will perish for the love of their sin. Before I was truly saved, I was lukewarm, and I thought I was saved. I went to church, prayed sometimes, talked about JESUS to others, and studied the Bible now and then. Sounds satisfactory doesn't it? On the other end I fornicated, lied, swore, and gossiped. I thought in my mind I could just repent and keep living in the sin I had grown accustomed to. I was wrong. We must walk in the ways of the LORD and when we fall short of the glory of GOD, we must repent. We have to at least try to do right by turning away from our sin. I understand it now, and once I became saved, I feel the beautiful love of JESUS. I have the peaceful power of the Holy Spirit within me, and I feel a Holy power I have never felt before. The Holy Spirit is filled with love for JESUS as you will be when you are filled with the Holy Spirit.

A beautiful image of Heaven! Wouldn't you prefer the beauty, peace, and serenity of heaven where our LORD sits on his throne? Or would you choose to burn in the abyss with the lying, deceitful, adversary because you love your sin? GOD gave us free will.

TESTIMONY #6
GOD'S DIVINE INTERFERENCE

Psalms 127:3 Lo, children are an heritage of the LORD; and the fruit of the womb is his reward

I was five years old and very sick at this time. I was just released from the hospital. I had spiked a fever so high, and it seemed unbreakable, so the doctors admitted me and I remained in the hospital for about a week. Ironically, they couldn't figure out what was wrong. They ran many tests but just could not diagnose me, but miraculously, I started getting better, so they discharged me to go home. Although I was home, it seemed I still had a long recovery. I was still very weak, and my grandmother made sure I was taking it easy. Now on this day my grandmother wanted to go shopping with her best friend Nina, but I was too weak to go along with them. So Nina suggested that her sixteen-year-old son Kelwin could babysit me because he was home from school for getting in trouble. I was only five years old, but I didn't have a good feeling about staying with Elwin. My grandmother, named Mona, and Nina were prancing around the house laughing and joking while Nina was getting ready for their shopping spree. Grandma turned her attention to Elwin to brief him about how to care for me as I was still very sick. My grandma tucked me away into the bed and said she would be back soon. She kissed my forehead, and then she turned and yelled,

"Nina, come on, let's go."

"I'm coming."

Nina yelled back. My grandma was still giving Kelwin instructions as she approached the door. She was rushing because she had to be back to prepare dinner before everyone came home from work and school. Kelwin was playing nice. He looked at me as I lay in the bed and said.

"Are you okay?"

I nodded my head yes.

"I'm going to take care of you, okay."

I said, "okay"

I was so innocent. Kelwin looked at me with this squeamish grin, that even as a child it made me uncomfortable, but I was too sick and weak to complain. I turned over to go to sleep as I heard my grandmother and Nina leaving, and just as I closed my eyes Kelwin was standing over me. So I turned over to face him, wondering what he was about to say. He stood there with that same squeamish grin as he said.

"You wanna play a game?"

I said, "*no, I don't feel very good!*"

"Aww come on it will be fun," Kelwin said as he got closer.

I began pleading with him to leave me alone. I was so sick, but now I was afraid . Kelwin knew I was weak and frail, Kelwin stood there still staring at me as he stripped off his clothes. Now again I was only 5 years old, and I didn't know what he was doing, but I knew it wasn't right. Kelwin took every piece of clothing he had OFF! He stood there looking at me like I was a full-fledged woman. When suddenly he heard a noise, he rushed to put his clothes back on thinking it was my grandmother and his mom, but it was only a false alarm. How I wish it were them. I was so afraid. Kelwin let off a sigh of relief, and came back to the room proceeding with taking off his clothes again. Mustering the strength, I sat up in bed, trying to figure out what was happening.

Kelwin looked at me and said, "lie back down."

So I reluctantly lay down. Kelwin climbed in the bed with me with not a shred of clothes on, and then he proceeded to take off my clothes. I said with my frail and weak voice.

"No! Please stop!"

But my pleas fell upon deaf ears. So, there I lay, a five-year-old helpless child, and didn't have a clue about what was happening. Kelwin climbed on the top of me and I could barely breathe because he was so big and I was so small, now I began to cry. Kelwin kissed and caressed my body as if I was a woman, yet I continued to plead with him to stop, but he seemed possessed. Nothing I said would stop him. Again I didn't know what he was doing, but I knew it DID NOT feel right. I had a naked sixteen-year-old on top of me at the age of five, and it most definitely wasn't a good feeling. It appeared as though the room stopped. Everything was quiet and still, like the calm before the storm. Kelwin started transforming into a wild beast on top of me, I was terrified, I screamed, when suddenly I heard the door and my grandmother's voice yelling Kelwin's name.

"Kelwin, where are you?"

Kelwin jumped up in surprise as he raced to put his clothes on before she came into the room. He could only put on his pants as he ran out of the room clutching his other clothes. My grandmother had forgotten her purse or GOD curved her memory to bring her back to save me, because my grandmother NEVER forgets her purse. Even to this day it is like her lifeline. Kelwin ran to the back of the house. This made my grandmother confused and very suspicious, as she ran into the bedroom to see me lying there crying and naked. By this time Nina came into the house wondering what was taking my grandmother so long. My grandmother was in total shock as she stood over me with her mouth dropped to the floor, yet she hadn't yet said a word. Suddenly, my grandma started screaming to the top of her lungs.

"Imma kill him! I will kill the little bastard!"

Nina yelled, "what's wrong? What happened?"

My grandmother had not a word to say as she reached into her purse and grabbed her .38 snub nose police special revolver as she hurled over Nina, still screaming

"I'm going to kill him!"

As Kelwin took off towards the back door and my grandmother

didn't waste any time opening fire as the whirlwind of bullets barely missed him. Nina screamed,

"NO! Mona please NO! Please don't kill my son, please I'm begging you Mona!"

My grandmother responded with a few more shots, as Kelwin barely got away. My grandmother ran to the backyard looking for him to get him, but he jumped that fence like an olympic star jumping hurdles. Miss Nina was still screaming and begging for her son's life. My grandmother came back into the house as she came straight to me to finish dressing me.

"Come on baby, let me get you out of here."

As she carried me out of the house she was ignoring Nina's crying as she looked at her and said,

"I'm going to find him and kill him."

She said her peace and walked out of the door, and Nina was still begging her. My grandmother carried me to the car, placed me inside, and we left. Nina knew my grandmother was a gun toting pistol and she would use it without hesitation. Grandma remained silent in the car, but I saw that look on her face, I knew she was mad. She looked at me and asked certain questions to assure just what Kelwin did or didn't do to me. I told my grandmother everything; it didn't go any further because my GOD sent my grandmother back to intervene. But he never got the chance to violate me. You see, sometimes, GOD may not come when we want him to, but he's always right on time. GOD allowed me to escape the abuse of a sexual predator, but there are many children who do not escape a sexual predator. Not all children have a gun toting grandmother to save them either. Each year, 1 in 3 girls are sexually abused before the age of 18. Also, 1 in 5 boys are sexually abused before the age of 18. GOD appointed us as the protector of our children. I believe this happened to me so I could one day testify to the world. Please protect our children, they are truly the last of the innocence. Here are some scriptures that tell you how GOD feels about people who hurt children.

Matthew 18:10 10 Take heed that ye despise not one of these little ones; for I say unto you, That in heaven their angels do always behold the face of my Father which is in heaven.

Mark 9:42 42 And whosoever shall offend one of these little ones that believe in me, it is better for him that a millstone were hanged about his neck, and he were cast into the sea.

Isaiah 49:25 25 But thus saith the Lord, Even the captives of the mighty shall be taken away, and the prey of the terrible shall be delivered: for I will contend with him that contendeth with thee, and I will save thy children.

You see, GOD'S love for our children is undeniable, and we as parents and adults should not only protect them, but hold them accountable when they are wrong. Kelwin got the beating of his life by my uncle, but his mother never held him accountable and as a result of that, Kelwin grew up to be a rapist, and murderer. Only the LORD knows what other demons possessed him. If he were held accountable when he did it to me, it may have saved others, I truly believe that he would have killed me after he raped me to keep me from telling. Thank GOD he saved me from being raped and murdered by this man. Kelwin ended up in prison.

JESUS loves us all, His love is so merciful and forgiving. He even loved Kelwin enough to give him a chance to straighten up his life. The truth is some people will not change and will not make it to Heaven.

Matthew 7:21-23 21 Not every man that saith unto me, "LORD, LORD, shall enter the Kingdom of Heaven. But he that doeth the will of my Father which is in Heaven. 22 Many will say to me on that day LORD, LORD, have we not prophesied in thy name? And in thy name have cast out devils? And in thy name done many wonderful works? 23 And then will I profess to them, I never knew you: depart from me, ye that works iniquity.

My brothers and sisters in CHRIST. Again I can't stress this enough, You will come across many false prophets, many deceivers, and many workers of iniquity. Be well and do NOT fall victim to the tricks of the adversary. The enemy is busy and ready to take as many as he can, for he knows his time is growing short. Let's go over the definition of iniquity so you will understand, because as you can see it is what caused JESUS to say, "depart from me workers of iniquity."

Iniquity- Injustice, unrighteousness, a deviation from rectitude, as the iniquity of war or as the iniquity of the SLAVE TRADE!

Iniquity comes in many forms as you can see. Henceforth, do not allow confusion to form. Iniquity is when we sin, but we do so of our own free will and even find pleasure in the very sin you are committing. Also, when your sinful nature is at a level where the Holy Spirit is no longer within you. Iniquity can also cause you to have no conscience. Iniquity is sin also, but worse because it is willfully and delightfully planned, yet you can sin by a mere accident. We have to change our hearts and our ways as well as repent daily for our sins and iniquities.

Isaiah 59:3 "For your hands are defiled with blood, and your fingers with iniquity: your lips have spoken lies, your tongue have muttered perverseness"

Psalm 51: 1-11 1 Have mercy upon me, O GOD according to thy lovingkindness: according unto the multitude of thy tender mercies blot out my transgressions. 2 Wash me thoroughly from mine iniquity, and cleanse me from my sin. 3 For I acknowledge my transgressions: and my sin is ever before me. 4 Against thee, thee only, have I sinned, and done this evil in thy sight: that thou mightest be justified when thou speakest, and be clear when thou judgeest. 5 Behold, I was shapen in iniquity; and in sin did my mother conceive me. 6 Behold, thou desirest truth in the inward parts: and in the hidden part thou shalt make me to know wisdom. 7 Purge me with hyssop, and I shall be clean: wash me, and I shall be whiter than snow. 8 Make me to hear joy and gladness; that the bones which thou hast broken may rejoice. 9 Hide thy face from my sins, and blot out all mine iniquities. 10 Create in me a clean heart, O GOD; and renew a right spirit in me.

TESTIMONY #7

GOD'S DESTINY

R omans 8:27 *GOD, the searcher of the heart, knows fully our longings, yet he also understands the desires of the Spirit, because the HOLY SPIRIT passionately pleads before GOD for us, his holy ones, in perfect harmony with GOD'S plan and our destiny.*

It's February of the year of 2020, the year the world changed forever. I'm browsing through my social media, avoiding stories about this deadly virus that's devastating China. I just didn't want to hear it, I just didn't know how to handle it. My cousin and I are browsing through Facebook looking for an old friend when low and behold, who do I see? The love of my life, Anthony.

"Wow," I said "I hadn't seen him in over 15 years,"

I told my cousin. So she looked at me and said.

"Message him."

I thought about it for a time, before I messaged him. I eventually did. I met him in 1997 and he was in prison at the time and I stood by his side for four long years while awaiting his release. My heart was with him and only him. We made so many plans, I even moved into a bigger house the closer it came time for his release. I wanted him to feel comfortable upon his release. I had two adolescent sons, ages three years old and eight years old. They were just as excited as I was as they had grown a bond with him over the years. We were all expecting his release. Anthony had been in prison for selling drugs. He came from a good two parent home with a devout Christian mom, but I guess he was just rebelling. I wanted to bring something different in his life. I felt we would be a power couple because we both had the same drive and ambition, only mine leaned more toward a legal and honest way of earning money. I wasn't saved then, but I had the spirit of GOD with me and I knew GOD, I just didn't know how to truly be saved. I knew the moment Anthony was released from that prison, I wanted to do everything I could to ensure he never went back. I met Anthony through mutual acquaintances, a couple we both knew. Anthony was friends with the man who I will call Dre and I was associated with the woman I will call Amy. One thing I noticed is Amy wasn't supportive of the relationship between Anthony and I. She said he was only using me and maybe he was. I didn't want to see it. I felt Amy meant well, but she just went about it the wrong way, but as time went on she worsened. I started getting a strong feeling she felt jealous. Everybody knew Anthony was a person who would make lots of money, and I started feeling like she just didn't want to see me happy or to see me win. I picked up a powerful jealousy spirit from her, now if you know anything about the spirit of jealousy, it is a very bad spirit. See what GOD Himself says about jealousy.

James 3:14-15, 14 But if you have bitter jealousy and selfish ambition in your hearts, do not boast and be false to the truth. 15 This is not the wisdom that comes down from above, but is earthly, unspiritual, and demonic.

So you see, GOD Himself despises the spirit of jealousy, and Amy was and still is full of this spirit. She just doesn't want to see me win or find happiness. I forgive her and I pray for her. Well, in 2001, it came time for Anthony's release from prison. He called me the morning he got out and told me to come and get him and Dre, the guy that introduced us, from his friend's house. I was so happy I could barely get my shoes on before leaving. I arrived at his friend's house to get them and we went out for breakfast. We had a laughing good ole time and then I dropped them both back at his friends' house. He promised he would come home to me that evening. I went home jumping up and down so thrilled. I told my sons he was coming home that evening. Well, evening came and no word from Anthony. Nightfall came so I called his friend's house and they said he left a long time ago. I was devastated. All I could do was sit there and cry and listen to Unbreak My Heart by Toni Braxton over and over. My sons felt the devastation as well. Needless to say, Anthony disappeared, and I never heard from him again for some years, but I never stopped loving him. I knew his own arrogance and the girl with the jealousy spirit had a lot to do with his betrayal. Yet, it was his decision to betray me in such a way and it changed my life forever. Which brings me back to this moment and sending him a message. I wanted even to this day, and I still loved him so very much. To my surprise he messaged me back. It began as small talk at first, and then I dove in.

"Why did you leave me like that? Why did you hurt me like that? Why didn't you love me?"

He said, "Hold on! Hold on! You are asking too many questions at one time!"

I said, "okay, I'm sorry."

So he said, "I'm sorry, I was just being a jerk and I have no excuse, but I'm sorry." WOW! I've been wanting an answer for over twenty years and every time I found him he would always run, so now he has faced me. That's all I wanted was closure, and he finally gave me the answers I wanted to hear. I didn't expect anything more, but Anthony was kind to me and he started sending a good morning text and calling me regularly, so I was like, okay. *Can I get the love of my life back? I would love to,* I thought. So I was all in. We talked on the phone for hours at a time and we grew close again, yet we were taking it slow. But I always made it clear I am still very much in love with him and wanted to marry him. All of this happened at the same time the Corona Virus hit the United States for the first time, and we were placed on quarantine all over the country. Anthony worked two jobs, and he worked them both the whole time we were in quarantine. He wasn't concerned about this virus but I was at first. The fear the enemy put in place worked on us all for a short while anyway, but not Anthony, he said,

"We gotta have faith."

And he was right. Anthony has always been a huge inspiration for me in many different ways. I lost my father to cancer, and my nephew to gun violence during this time. It was really hard for me. Anthony was there for me at first, but for some reason he started to change. He became insulting and seemed to have a lack of empathy. He never was emotional, but he was a bit cold. I knew he'd been through a lot throughout the years, and I felt that had a role to play in it. He started saying, I was surrounded by drama, and I thought *well I didn't know the death of my loved ones was drama,* but it was surely NOT my DRAMA, but it was my LOSS. I then noticed he was very low on compassion. And then there were our spiritual beliefs, I'm a follower of Christ JESUS, and Anthony is a skeptic who's always questioning GOD. He is one of those people who based everything on facts and proof. Almost like a Scientologist or an Atheist, and he also follows a popular brother online in whose name I will not mention. This man isn't religious, and isn't a follower of CHRIST. I believe Anthony has adopted a lot of his warped beliefs. The Bible speaks of ungodly men and their hard speeches against the LORD. The LORD will deal with them as they are leading people away from GOD. Anthony says he believes in GOD but he just has questions about GOD, or for GOD, yet GOD's children know we are not to question GOD. You might not like how he answers you. Anthony said part of the Bible is fictional, but he just doesn't trust GOD's supernatural powers. He has no spirituality and continues living in the flesh, and this has led us to many debates. But no matter what, I love Anthony very much, and I pray for GOD to come in and give him a clean heart and fill him with a righteous spirit. I felt GOD could fix our differences but in,

2 Corinthians 6:14 it says Do not be unequally yoked with unbelievers. For what partnership has righteousness with lawlessness? Or what fellowship has light with darkness? But I know the LORD is merciful and loving, and I felt Anthony still had a chance because he says he believes in GOD, but he's confused about a lot of things. Which can happen when you listen to mere men with their ideas and theories, in their hard speeches. I call them tools of Satan, used to lure people away from salvation with CHRIST JESUS. On this day I conversed with Anthony via phone and I gave him one of my life's testimonies, he listened. He is great about listening, but sometimes he doesn't hear things how he should hear them, but after this testimony he had one word and that was WOW! I smiled because I finally got through to a skeptic. I can tell my testimony had an influence on him.But after that I didn't hear from him for about four days. I noticed he was doing this when he started to get too close to me. He would stay away a week or so, and it left a bad taste in my mouth, and made me have flashbacks. GOD is so amazing and works in mysterious ways. You see, I saw the effect my testimony took on Anthony. God knew if I could reach him I could reach many more, and the Holy Spirit told me to write a book of my testimonies, so I listened, obeyed and immediately started writing. You see GOD used Anthony, a skeptic to inspire me to use the gift he blessed me with. Writing and writing something that could help lead millions to salvation with JESUS CHRIST. Anthony didn't even realize he had been used by the same GOD he questions. I was so excited about the book I couldn't wait to begin writing. Once I started, I couldn't stop. I started in April and it's July and I'm almost done. I said the power of GOD helped me write this book and I believe in it's anointment, which leads me to the rest of this testimony. Oh yeah, I saved the best for last. Please know at this time I am saved , and I am living for CHRIST JESUS, but this wasn't always my walk in life. I had to go through some trials to get here. Once again while scrolling through Facebook I came across a celebrity rapper from Manchester, UK who was so talented I couldn't stop watching his videos. He was rapping about GOD which really caught my attention, and yes he's very handsome; I might add. Well, for some strange reason I decided to reach out to him, I didn't think he would respond like most celebrities don't, but he did. His name is Rio Nelson, and he's an exceptional man. He's truly my brother in Christ. Rio answered my message, which read:

Hello you are very talented and I really like your music and you now have an American fan, or something like that. And he was so humble and appreciative. So we then started talking about GOD, and he told me he had just recently become saved. He didn't have many people he could talk to about the LORD, so we really hit it off because we were equally yoked. We can talk about GOD and never get uncomfortable with it. So I supported all his music and shared his content, as a matter-of fact Facebook dubbed me his #1 fan. We were out of touch for about two weeks, because I was busy dealing with Anthony and writing my book. I also forgave Amy and let her back in my life, which was a huge mistake. I thought in time people would change, but I was mistaken. She still had the same deviant, jealous spirit. Originally after the third testimony of the book, I was going to end there, but the Holy Spirit told me to keep writing, and I did. So I needed 5 people to read the book so I could get their excerpts. For some reason I reached out to Rio to be a reader, as his opinion is very important to me, and he gladly accepted. At first, I think he forgot and I had to remind him, but I knew he was very busy so I didn't want to press the issue.

Anthony was the 1st person I sent my book to read. He lied and told me he read it and couldn't give an actual opinion because he didn't really read it and I   didn't even confront him on it, but that hurt my feelings. It seems Anthony is good at hurting me if nothing else, but I kept praying GOD would change him. Rio on the other hand not only read my book but after each testimony he gave me feedback. Rio has been GOD sent in my life. Keep reading and you all will agree. Rio Nelson was raised by his grandmother, Mabel Nelson in Manchester, England. Rio describes his grandmother as an angel, and a prayer warrior. He started rapping at a very young age, he had a friend named T-fizzle who introduced him to the art of rapping, which they call grime and rap. Rio took the art of grime and rap to another level. He's very driven, ambitious, and goal oriented. He's worked with some big artists in the United States like Nas, Busta Rhymes, and Rick Ross. But Rio took about a four year break from music because of some trials and tribulations he was going through or shall I say that GOD was taking him through. Sometimes GOD will break you down to build you back up in His likeness, At the time it may seem to be hurtful or painful, but there's a greater good for the outcome. Like Rio, he was at the top of his career before GOD intervened to redirect his life. GOD always has a plan, we can try to plan our lives, but like someone wise once said:

"If you want to make GOD laugh, tell him your plans."

One thing we should all remember is no matter how you are living your life, the LORD always knows your heart. Some people do good deeds and have cruel hearts, while others live in the ways of the world yet have good hearts. Rio Nelson has a good heart, and

GOD has acknowledged it, so he broke Rio down to rebuild him again. Rio was at the top of his career when he and his manager mutually decided to part ways. This caused some grief for the talented rapper. It was only the start of a plethora of events that will cause his long break in music, and he rapped about these events in his song "Adversities." Rio placed all his pain in this song, so much that whoever is listening will feel his pain. Rio, the father of two sons, is an excellent father who loves his boys very much. In 2016 he faced many adversities. He said it was the hardest year for him ever. He was in and out of court fighting for his sons, suffering financial hardships, suffering a harsh break up, and all of this caused some anxiety and minor depression issues. Rio felt he had nowhere to turn. He turned to GOD, and this changed his life for the better.

"It's spiritual warfare," Rio says.

He is correct, we live in spiritual warfare every day. In Romans, it explains, we can NOT live in the flesh, we MUST live in the spirit.

Romans 8:6 For to set the mind on the flesh is death, but to set the mind on the Spirit is life and peace.

Rio gave his life to JESUS CHRIST the summer of 2019 and says that he is now being led by the HOLY SPIRIT. Through meditation and prayer the HOLY SPIRIT helps him showcase his talent and music. When I asked him if he knew GOD'S purpose for him he stated:

"I believe GOD wants me to be an ambassador to help people get on the right side of the fence, I believe I will go worldwide helping people."

Rio has an enormous heart and a genuine love for people. GOD saw that when he wasn't saved and that's why he had to break him down and rebuild him. Now that I've given a back story on Rio, let's fast forward back to when we met. Again we met on Facebook after I saw some of his work and reached out to him. Rio and I immediately connected on a spiritual level, and had the best conversations about GOD. We are equally yoked in that area. We developed a very close bond and have become really good friends. And no I wasn't trying to date him and he wasn't trying to date me. We are really close and Rio has been very supportive of me and this book the whole time I have been writing it. and we have a bond that's out of this world. I genuinely just loved him as my brother in CHRIST. I posted on my Facebook for help with my book cover design, and Rio jumped right on it and had it done in no time. There were days as I was writing, I felt discouraged, or life's happenings had me down and out, and it's like Rio feels my spirit and I feel his. He knows just when to send me that motivation video or just the right words to say to motivate and encourage me and I have the same effect on him. Well, I'm sure you all are wondering *how she could have this kind of bond with him and not find him attractive or fall in love with* him? Well, I fell in love with Rio, I mean how could I not fall in love with him. He's handsome, ambitious, loving, caring, supportive, and most important of all, he's GOD fearing. So yes, I fell in love with him but I had to hide it because he was in a relationship and I didn't want to be disrespectful. He was not showing any signs that he found me attractive in that way. So I have remained just a friend and a sister in CHRIST to him. I always thought I couldn't truly love any man outside of Anthony, but Rio stole my heart, and I love him in a way that I don't even understand, I mean it's like I love him in every way. I love him like my brother in CHRIST; I love him like my friend, and I'm in love with him. It's a love I never experienced before and I will always be here for him no matter what. So I selflessly suppressed my love for him, which is hard and hurtful, but rather than lose him completely I complied. I will always respect his feelings and If we are only friends forever, I'm okay with it. That just means GOD has someone else to place in my life as a husband and life partner. GOD has put us together for a reason and I believe it's more than one reason. The old saying goes, A reason for a season, sometimes it's a short season, sometimes it's a long season, but it's always a reason. Whatever the reason is, I am following GOD's lead and trusting in him throughout this entire journey. Rio found a friend in me for life, and I have found one in him. If the only way I can be in his life is as a friend then I will take it, because he's a very good friend. So you see, GOD removed Anthony yet again and replaced him with someone very special named Rio. GOD also showed me why he removed Anthony the first time, when I thought Anthony turned his back on me and left me. It was actually GOD removing him because when they released Anthony from prison the 1st time he went back to his old ways. Which caused him and the woman he was with at the time, to both get into big trouble. You see, GOD did not want that for me so he removed him out of my life. JESUS is so exceptional and incredible that sometimes he actually protects us from our own selves. You see, GOD knew Anthony would not be the support factor I needed while writing this book, because He saw Anthony's heart and heard his thoughts. So he sent Rio as an amazing friend and supporter, all while removing Anthony yet once again. Sweet

JESUS, won't GOD do it! The LORD has his own plan for our lives; we aren't here for our own purpose but for GOD's purpose. I placed some helpful Bible scriptures below about GOD's destiny for us. I hope my life's testimonies can lead whosoever shall read this book to SALVATION with JESUS CHRIST.

Jeremiah 29:11 For I know the plans I have for you, declares the LORD, plans for welfare and not for evil, to give you a future and a hope.

Habakkuk 2:3 For still the vision awaits the appointed time, it hastens to the end--it will not lie. If it seems slow, wait for it; it will surely come; it will not delay.

John 16:33 I have said these things to you, that in me you may have peace. In the world you will have tribulation, But take heart, I have overcome the world.

Jeremiah 17:10 "I the LORD search the heart and test the mind, to give every man according to his ways, according to the fruit of his deeds.

Galatians 6:7 Do not be deceived: GOD is not mocked, for whatever one sows, that will he also reap.

Matthew 22:37 JESUS said unto him, Thou shalt love the LORD thy GOD with all thy heart, and with all thy soul, and with all thy mind.

AFTERWORD II

I t's July 2020, the year the world changed forever. In January 2020, I sat staring at the news which I very seldom watch, while the major topic was the Coronavirus. I didn't have a tremendous concern for it then; I thought to myself: *Well, it's way in China, surely the U.S. government will not allow them to gain entry into the U.S. to bring it over here.* I truly thought our government would protect us. Well I was terribly wrong. Here we stand in a world of chaos, with a President who appears to be a bigot, and a racist. The virus is spreading rapidly as the greed of the politicians force them to re-open the economy. Racism is at an all-time high with racist police officers murdering African Americans, and medical racism. People are out of work as the governors of the states lift moratoriums which allows their evictions and their utilities to be shut off. African Americans are tired of being discriminated against, and murdered for the color of their skin. Decent white people are joining them in protest because of the outrage at racial violence at this point. Protest all over the world starts in light of the murder of of George Floyd, a black man who was murdered by a racist police officer. The whole world appears to be tired of racist America, as protest sparks all over the world. There's looting and rioting amidst the protest by non-protestors deemed to make the protestors look guilty, along with the few protestors who actually were rioting and looting. The LGBTQ+ Community aligned with the Black Lives Matter group to form an allegiance. Child sex trafficking is growing at an alarming rate and nothing seems to be get done to stop it, they are starving in Africa as their government hoards the money. Rich eugenists are trying to play GOD and manipulate the virus for population control. China seems to be cooking up the next virus to unleash on the world again, and Russia is quiet. Just sitting back watching and waiting for the right time to move in and take control over the falling nation of the United States of America. I mean, what in the name of JESUS is happening in this world today? Well, let's talk about it. Let's start with President Trump, yes he's probably a racist and a bigot, but he believes in GOD and wants nothing to do with his elite devil worshipping counterparts. You see, now we will look at this from a spiritual perspective, because we are in spiritual warfare, good vs. evil. You see, GOD will use the very people we wouldn't think he would use to fulfil his purpose. President Trump has been the one man blocking the evildoers. He pulled funds from the W.H.O. (World Health Organization), he's the one exposing them for not using the drug combination that could potentially stop the virus from killing people. He's the one that will not approve of the vaccine until the proper amount of testing has been performed. President Trump is fighting a battle bigger than racism. GOD is using him to fight for humanity and this is why GOD gave him the position in office because if you will remember he lost the election. It was GOD who put him in office. The elite Bill Gates concocted a plan to place RFID chips in people's hands *(mark of the beast)* if they do not take the vaccine which just might slowly kill people. Remember Bill Gates is a eugenist and wants to control the population. These people have a very evil agenda. President Trump announced there will not be forced vaccines or forced microchips administered to the citizens of America. President Trump, as strange as it sounds, I believe is being used by GOD and he desperately needs our prayers. Let's refer to the scripture in the Holy Bible for this:

Proverbs 16:4 The LORD has made everything for its purpose, Yes, even the wicked for the day of trouble.

GOD is in control of all things, and those who are not spiritually connected to GOD will not see or understand what's happening.

2 Corinthians 4:4 In their case the GOD of this world has blinded the minds of the unbeliever, to keep them from seeing the light of the gospel of the glory of CHRIST JESUS, who is the image of GOD.

So it's best to get to know the LORD, get saved, learn and study the word so you will know how to fight the beast. The Bible prophecies will and already are coming to pass. The enemy is out to seek kill and destroy. Satan is the reason GOD sent his Son. See it in scripture.

John 3:8 Whoever makes a practice of sinning is of the devil, for the devil has been sinning from the beginning.

The reason the Son of GOD appeared was to destroy the works of the devil.

You see everything that has happened, is happening, and will happen is in the same Holy Bible some try to discredit. It's nothing but a wicked, deceitful scheme of the adversary.

1 Peter 5:8 Be sober-minded; be watchful. Your adversary the devil prowls around like a roaring lion, seeking someone to devour.

James 4:7 Submit yourselves therefore to GOD. Resist the devil, and he will flee from you.

We have to accept JESUS in our lives and stay prayed up drowned in faith. Do you know what this chaos in the world is? It is the adversary! He is busy, for he knows his time will come soon. For every sin has a demon attached, the world is full of sin and evil. That is why there's so much mayhem and confusion. GOD'S people must come together because we will be attacked, imprisoned and even killed. We will have to come together as the LORD wants us too, so we may fight and survive. The prophecy of the Bible is coming to pass. Time is growing short. The rapture can happen any day. Do you want to go in the rapture? Or do you want to be left behind to fight the spirits and principalities of the beast? I don't know about you, but I would much rather go in the rapture unless the LORD called me to stay behind and help the lost get to CHRIST! Let's see what GOD says about the rapture in scripture:

1 Thessalonians 4:15-17 15 For this we say unto you by the word of the LORD, that we which are alive and remain unto the coming of the LORD shall not prevent them which are asleep.

16 For the LORD himself shall descend from heaven with a shout, with the voice of the archangel, and with the trump of GOD: and the dead in CHRIST shall rise first: 17 Then we which are alive and remain shall be caught up together with them in the clouds, to meet the LORD in the air: and so shall we ever be with the LORD. 18 Wherefore comfort one another with these words.

You see, the dead will rise and the living will be swooped up in the clouds along with the dead to meet Our LORD JESUS CHRIST in the clouds. There is great instruction prophesied in none other than the "HOLY BIBLE." We have been blinded and controlled by the media, sports, music, television, and celebrity gossip. All while the beast is preparing to rise. What will you do when they demand you to take the rfid chip? If you refuse, you will not be able to buy food, pay bills, and live in the way of which you've been accustomed to, all in the name of JESUS! What will you sacrifice? And will you trust in the LORD? These are all very valid questions we should ask ourselves. We must grow our food or we will starve, and more than anything we have to trust in JESUS that he will be there for his people. I must emphasize and plead with you to study your Bible, and remain informed. GOD says most of His people will be destroyed due to lack of knowledge. Remember, the current situation is only temporary, and the outcome is the greatest reward, which is eternal life and love with our savior, JESUS CHRIST. Again, will you go in the rapture? Or will you get left behind for the 7 years of Tribulation where there will be great suffering and the Anti-Christ will have temporary power. After the 7 Years of Tribulation CHRIST will come back with His Saints that he rose from the dead, and the living in which he called up in the rapture. As loving and merciful as he has been, he wont be very loving upon his return, they will see his wrath and it won't be pretty. He will come to destroy the wicked, to judge the non believers, to destroy the evil minions and the wicked adversary. Then there will be peace on Earth, no more sickness, evil, or wicked deeds. I know some of you who read this book will not be saved in the name of JESUS CHRIST. It's your choice, GOD gave us free will. I pray most who have read it, will give your life over to CHRIST. Go back to the middle of this book and say the prayer to surrendering your life to JESUS CHRIST. GOD led me to write this book, and I know some of you have never read or studied a Bible. So I have included a very important Bible study to help you begin your journey of learning the wisdom and knowledge of GOD'S prophecy. Along with Bible scriptures from the KJV of the HOLY BIBLE. May GOD Bless you my brothers and sisters. JESUS CHRIST loved you enough to give his life for you. Love yourself enough to give your life to JESUS CHRIST. IN JESUS NAME. AMEN.

BONUS: BIBLE STUDY.

- What did Jesus' disciples ask him in private?

Matthew 24: 1-3   1 And JESUS went out and departed from the temple: and his disciples came to him for to shew him the buildings of the temple.   2 And JESUS said unto them, See ye not all these things? Verily I say unto you, There shall not be left here one stone upon another, that shall not be thrown down.   3 And as he sat upon the mount of Olives, the disciples came unto him privately, saying, Tell us, when shall these things be? And what shall be the sign of thy coming, and of the end of the world?

- What was the first answer JESUS gave the disciples?

Matthew 24: 4-5   4 And Jesus answered, Take heed that no man deceives you. 5 For many shall come in my name, saying I am CHRIST; and shall deceive many

- In Matthew 24: 6-8 Name the events that JESUS calls "the beginning of sorrows"? And have these events already occurred today?

Matthew 24: 6-8 6 And ye shall hear of wars and rumors of wars: see that ye be not troubled: for all these things must come to pass, but the end is not yet, 7 For nation shall rise against nation, and kingdom against kingdom: and there shall be famines, and pestilences, and earthquakes, in divers places. 8 All these are the beginning of sorrows.

- Then shall they deliver you up to be

_____, and shall _____ you: and ye shall be _____ of all nations for _____.

Matthew 24:9 Then shall they deliver you up to be afflicted, and shall kill you: and ye shall be hated of all nations for my name's sake.

- And then shall many be _____, and shall _____ one another, and shall _____ one another.

Matthew 24:10 And then shall many be offended, and shall betray one another, and shall hate one another.

- Who will rise and deceive many?

Matthew 24:11 And many false prophets shall rise, and shall deceive many.

- And because _ _ _ _ _ _ shall _ _ _ _ _ _ , the love of many shall be _ _ _ _ _ _ _

Matthew 24:12 And because iniquity shall abound, the love of many shall wax cold.

- Who did JESUS say will be saved in the end?

Matthew 24:13 But he that shall endure unto the end, the same shall be saved.

- What did JESUS say will happen, that will be the sign before the end?

Matthew 24:14 And this gospel of the kingdom shall be preached in all the world for a witness unto all nations; and then shall the end come.

- What does JESUS instruct us to do when you see the abomination of desolation spoken of by Daniel the prophet?

Matthew 24:15 When ye therefore shall see the abomination of desolation, spoken of by Daniel the prophet, stand in the Holy place, (Whoso readeth, let him understand)

- *What specific warnings did JESUS give us to abide by in the next few verses of Matthew?*

Matthew 24: 16-18   16 Then let them which be in Judae'-a flee into the mountains. 17 Let him which is on the housetop not come down to take anything out of his house: 18 Neither let him which is in the field return back to take his clothes.

- Matthew 24 is Jesus' prophecy he gave to his disciples about the end and his return. Read Matthew 24: 19-22 and take important notes for the prophesied instructions from our

Messiah, and study these notes as reminders.

Notes--

Matthew 24: 19-22 19 And woe unto them are with child, and to them that give suck in those days! 20 But pray ye that your flight be not in the winter, neither on the sabbath day: 21 For then shall be great tribulation, such as was not since the beginning of the world to this time, no, nor ever shall be.

22 And except those days should be shortened, there should no flesh be saved: but for the elect's sake those days shall be shortened.

What warnings does JESUS want us to take heed to about false prophets and deceivers?

Matthew 24: 23-24 23 Then if any man shall say unto you, Lo, here is CHRIST, or there; believe it not. 24 For there shall arise false CHRISTS, and false prophets, and shall shew great signs, and wonders; insomuch that, if it were possible, they shall deceive the very elect.

- What warning comes after the word "Behold" each time in

Matthew 24:25-26. And why?

Matthew 24: 25-26   25   Behold, I have told you before. 26 Wherefore if they shall say unto you, Behold, he is in the desert; go not forth; behold, he is in the secret chambers; believe it not.

- For Matthew 24: 27-28 we will have a discussion, Matthew 24: 28 is one of the most controversial verses in the Bible, at least for some. There are a lot of people who will take and misconstrue the words of the Bible, to mislead others. Do not be misled. Let's have a discussion below:

Matthew 24:27 For as the lightning cometh out of the east, and shineth even unto the west; so shall also the coming of the Son of man be.

Discussion: Well, one thing we know is the LORD works in mysterious ways, and what I'm coming to learn the more I study the Bible, he speaks in mysterious ways as well. The spirit of discernment can help you with that. How do you get the spirit of discernment? Simply pray for it. You see the closer you build your relationship with GOD, the more you will understand the Bible. This verse is speaking about the triumphant return of JESUS after the 7 years of tribulation, which will also be during the time of the Anti- Christ and the false prophets he has been warning us about in the whole first half of Matthew 24. He will come with the lightning from the east to the west. There will be no mistake when he comes, it will be powerful, glorious, and magnificent. Remember the seven years tribulation comes after the rapture in which he comes like a thief in the night for his Saints. Let's now discuss the one that has been really misconstrued by many.

Matthew 24:28 For wheresoever the carcase is, there will the vultures be gathered together.

In this one we will use parallel passages, which are passages from another part of the Bible about the same event. This is very helpful to know when you are studying the Bible. It's nice to have another view coming from another book in the Bible, helping to paint a clear picture of the event, as you will now see in this discussion. So the 1st parallel passage I would like to use is in *Luke 17:37 And they answered and said unto him, Where, Lord? And he said unto them, Wheresoever the body is, thither will the eagles be gathered together,* Now as you can see Matthew and Luke share the same testimony about the same event, but it's in their own words. Now let's go to the 3rd parallel passage which explains this event in greater detail. *Revelation 19: 17-19 And I saw angel standing in the sun, and he cried out with a loud voice, saying to all the birds that fly in midheaven, "Come assemble for the great supper of GOD; in order that you may eat the flesh of kings and the flesh of commanders and the flesh of mighty men and the flesh of horses and of those who sit on them and the flesh of all men, both free men and slaves, and small and great." And I saw the beast and the kings of the earth and their armies, assembled to make war against him who sat upon the horse, and against his army. And the rest were killed with the sword which came from the mouth of him who sat upon the horse, and all the birds were filled with their* flesh." So what did you all get from that? Him who sat upon the horse is CHRIST JESUS. The angels summoned the vultures to come eat upon the flesh of the wicked that are about to be judged and slaughtered by CHRIST JESUS. Do you now see how the parallel passages work? The Holy Bible is truly an amazing book, just like its author. "The vultures are the judgement of the wicked, and the carcase is the body of the wicked," (Robert Gundry). Matthew 24 is a chapter, I want you all to study well. It is JESUS' own prophecy of his return. Remember, the scripture describes the "beast," who is the beast? The beast is the antichrist. In Revelation 19 it clearly says, the beast will be present as well as the wicked, the kings of the earth and their armies, as JESUS opens his mouth and releases the swords to destroy the wicked and the False Christ. Please take notes and study well, because these things that are prophesied by the MESSIAH thousands of years ago are now coming to pass right before our eyes. The problem is the world is deceived and most can't see the prophecy unfold.

Notes--

For Matthew 24: 29-31 we will have another discussion. These discussions are important to help you all reach the understanding of this chapter. Your life could depend on it.

Matthew 24: 29 Immediately after the tribulation of those days shall the sun be darkened, and the moon shall not give her light, and the stars shall fall from heaven, and the powers of the heavens shall be shaken.

Discussion: Now remember the previous discussion, we used parallel passages from Revelation 19 to describe Matthew 24:28. Verse 29 is now going to give us the prophecy from JESUS of the same event. After the 7 year tribulation JESUS describes the events that will take place. The sun shall be darkened, the moon will not give off light, the stars will fall from the heavens, and the power coming from heaven will shake the heavens. Jesus is letting us know his return will be noticed and it will be more powerful than we can imagine and we will see wonders never before seen.

Matthew 24:30 And then shall appear the sign of the Son of man in heaven: and then shall all the tribes of the earth mourn, and they shall see the Son of man coming in the clouds of heaven with power and great glory.

Let's talk about the sign. What do you think the sign will be? An array of colorful lights maybe? Or maybe a rolling ball of thunder? Or maybe the same sign that was used in previous biblical history to announce JESUS, or the divine presence of GOD, which is the Shekhinah Glory. What does this mean? *Shekinah Glory- is the english transliteration of a Hebrew word meaning "dwelling" or "settling" and denotes the dwelling or settling of the divine presence of GOD. {R Wikipedia}* However the good LORD decides to do it, it will not go unnoticed. Now let's talk about the tribes of the earth JESUS speaks about that will mourn. Now some scholars and theologians have different views on this passage, Some felt JESUS is coming to take vengeance on the tribes of people in the land of Judea, and they will mourn at his coming for fear of his judgement and punishment that's about to come upon them, now part of that is true but look at the passage real good. JESUS says "and then shall all the tribes of the earth mourn." Does that sound like he's saying only the land of Judea to you? No he's not, he said, ALL the tribes of the EARTH will mourn because judgement and punishment is coming upon them. The wicked have run out of time, and they know it. The world has made wrong right and right wrong. JESUS will be back to put it all back in the order it belongs. Right is right and wrong is wrong. They will see the Son of man coming out of the clouds of heaven with great power and he will be a force that can't be reckoned with. And he shall send his angels to sound off with the great trumpet amidst his return. Save yourself people, accept CHRIST JESUS as your LORD and Savior. We are running out of time. The Bible tells us what we can and can't do, but just like the tribes of Judea, man have been stubborn, rebellious, and disobedient to GOD. Many of those have even went so far as to discredit the Bible or remove passages from it to continue their life of filth and sin. Change your ways, repent, and get saved, please my brothers and sisters. GOD loved us enough to give his only Son's life for us all. Let's show him as much love and respect as we can, lest you will be one of the people who mourn at JESUS' return to slay the wicked and let the vultures feast on their bodies. Take notes on this discussion and keep them as a reminder of what's to come. Spread the word, and teach your children the ways of the LORD.

Notes---

JESUS loved to speak in parables, what did the parable mean in Matthew 24:32-33 and how did he compare it with his return?

Matthew 24:32   Now learn a parable of the fig tree; When his branch is yet tender, and putteth forth leaves, ye know the summer is nigh: 33 So likewise ye, when ye shall see all of these things, know that it is near, even at the doors.

- What does JESUS say about Heaven, earth and fulfillment in Matthew 24: 34-35?

Matthew 24:34-35   34 Verily I say unto you, This generation shall not pass, till all these things be fulfilled. 35 Heaven and earth shall pass away, but my words shall not pass away.

- What man knows the day or the hour the son of man is coming?

Matthew 24:36   But of that day and hour knoweth no man, no not the angels of heaven, but my father only.

- How does JESUS compare Noah's ark and the great flood to his second coming in Matthew 24:37-39?

Matthew 24:37-39   37 But as the days of No'-e were, so shall also the coming Son of man be.   38 For as in the days that were before the flood they were eating and drinking, marrying and giving in marriage, until the day that No'-e entered into the ark.   39 And knew not until the flood came, and took them all away; so shall also the coming of the Son of man be.

How does JESUS explain the rapture in Matthew 24:40-41?

Matthew 24: 40   Then shall two be in the field; the one shall be taken, and the other left.   41 Two women shall be grinding at the mill; the one shall be taken, and the other left.

- How does JESUS compare the hour of his return to that of the "goodman of the house parable in Matthew 24: 42-44?" Write a breakdown for your notes to keep as a reminder.

Matthew 24: 42-44   42   Watch therefore: for ye know not what hour your LORD doth come?   43   But know this, that if the goodman of the house had known in what watch the thief would come, he would have watched, and would not have suffered his house to be broken up.   44   Therefore be ye also ready: for on such an hour as ye think not the SON of man cometh.

- Now that we are upon the completion of the Bible study, we will end with a discussion for JESUS' last parable of Matthew for Matthew 24:45-51. Please take note:

Matthew 24: 45   Who then is a faithful and wise servant, whom his LORD hath made ruler over his household, to give them meat in due season?   46 Blessed is that servant, whom his LORD when he cometh shall find so doing.   47 Verily I say unto you, That he shall make him ruler over all his goods.   48 But and if that evil servant shall say in his heart, My LORD delayeth his coming.

49 And shall begin to smite his fellow servants, and to eat and drink with the drunken; 50 The LORD of that servant shall come in a day where he looketh not for him, and in a hour that he is not aware of, 51 And shall cut him asunder, And appoint him his portion with the hypocrites: there shall be weeping and gnashing of teeth.

Discussion: Now this is one of the LORD'S more difficult parables, yet do not be discouraged my brothers and sisters. Pray for understanding of the Bible and he will give it to you. Join a Bible study group, they have them online now. Now let's get to the discussion. The LORD speaks first of the faithful and wise servant whom his LORD has put in charge of the household. Now some would argue that JESUS is referring to the nation of Israel and the faithful and wise servant who is in charge is the leadership of Israel and his LORD is who is in charge over all. The good servant will be blessed being in charge over all the goods. My dispute is though this is a parable, I know Jesus will not only judge the good servants of the nation of Israel, but he will judge the good servants of all nations. Let's look at one of the parallel passages for this verse. *Matthew 25:21*

His LORD said unto him, well done, thou good and faithful servant: thou hast been faithful over a few things, I will make thee ruler over many things: enter thou into the joy of thy LORD.

Luke 16:10 He that is faithful in that which is least is faithful also in much: and he that is unjust in the least is unjust also in much. So the good and faithful servants are those who follow in CHRIST, keep GOD'S commandments, and live by the word of GOD, the Holy Bible. This parable highlights that CHRIST has warned us (his servants) of his return. He has sent his prophets and chosen ones to warn the world of his return as well. Are you all with me? Let's review in simple form. We are the servants, the parable explains that the good servants will be rewarded and reap the harvest of the good seeds sown upon his return. Now for the servants who choose to ignore the prophets and the warnings of the return of CHRIST, and not knowing their own scripture, (lack of knowledge) *mostly by their own free will, for their own need of doing what they like to do and not doing what was right. Well, the LORD calls them in verse 48 and 49 the evil servant who will smite his fellow servants and get drunk with the drunken. Does this sound familiar? Just look all around you. The* world is full of evil servants that choose to ignore the warnings of the MESSIAH coming back to judge them, which will reap great consequences. Upon JESUS' return the world will be judged and the faithful will receive the kingdom and the unfaithful will not receive the Kingdom, instead they will receive condemnation. Which will you decide to be? A faithful or an unfaithful servant?

Notes--

Thank you for participating my brothers and sisters in CHRIST. I pray you find your Salvation with JESUS CHRIST, and may we all celebrate one day as saints in heaven. May GOD bless you, and may GOD keep you.

Your Sister in CHRIST

LaDon

THE AMAZING PROPHECIES
OF DANIEL

The amazing prophecy of the coming of JESUS CHRIST

Daniel's entire seventy year period of ministry while in babylonian captivity was his life. While held captive he was brought to Babylon at the age of 16. Daniel, amongst others were picked by King Nebuchadnez'zar for government service. The King requested children who had no blemish, who were highly favored, skillful in all wisdom, cunning in knowledge, and who had understanding of science. These would be the ones who had the ability to stand in the King's Palace and teach. Daniel would become GOD'S prophetic mouthpiece, to the Gentiles and the Jews, declaring GOD'S present and eternal purpose. Daniel was given visions and dreams by GOD that showed GOD'S guidance, intervention, and power in the affairs of men. The name Dani'el means, "GOD is my judge," in the Greek form. So how did Daniel gain favor from GOD? Well let's go to the scripture for that answer. The King appointed a daily portion of the King's meat and wine to all the young men who were chosen to teach and stand in the King's palace, but Daniel did not want to defile himself with the meat and wine.

Daniel 1: 8-10   8 But Daniel purposed in his heart that he would not defile himself with the King's meat, nor with the wine which he drank: therefore he requested of the prince of the eunuchs that he may not defile himself.   9 Now GOD had brought Daniel into favour and tender love with the prince of the eunuchs.   10 And the prince of the eunuchs said unto Daniel, I fear my Lord the King, who hath appointed your meat and your drink: for why should he see your faces worse liking than the children of your sort? Then shall ye make me endanger my head to the King.

Daniel asked if he and three other valued servants could only eat vegetables and water for ten days to prove the meat and wine was a defilement, as well as prove to them that the vegetables and water were better for them. He asked to be compared to the other children who ate the meat and drank the wine after the ten day period, thus giving birth to the famous Daniel fast.

Daniel 1:12-16   12 Prove thy servants, I beseech thee, ten days;and let them give us vegetables to eat and water to drink.   13 Then let our countenances be looked upon before thee, and the countenance of the children that eat of the portion of the King's meat: and as thou seest, deal with thy servants.   14 So he consented to them in this matter, and proved them ten days.   15 And at the end of the ten days their countenances appeared fairer and fatter in flesh than all the children which did eat the portion of the King's meat.   16 Thus Mel'-zar took away the portion of their meat, and wine that they should drink; and gave them vegetables.

GOD was so pleased with these four children he gave them knowledge and skill in all learning and wisdom, and Daniel had understanding in all visions and dreams.

Now that we have the understanding of how and why Daniel gained favour from GOD, we will now witness the greatest testament of prophecies of the first coming of JESUS CHRIST in the OLD TESTAMENT.

Many have criticized the new testament and it's accuracy, which the main subject many non-believers want to challenge is the death and resurrection of JESUS CHRIST. It is only deception of the enemy. If the enemy can get people to doubt JESUS the MESSIAH died for their sins then they won't repent, if they don't believe and repent then their destination is hell. Religion is a powerful tool of the enemy. Look at the Muslim religion who calls JESUS a prophet. Look at the Roman Catholic religion who prays and worships Mary, Look at the believers in the pagan gods who believe JESUS lives in the sun and didn't die on the cross. Look at the Buddhist who praise and worship a graven image. What do they all have in common? They all denounce JESUS CHRIST as the Son of GOD. It is their common denominator and the enemy is laughing his hooves off at how gullible mankind is . It is no coincidence all of these religions denounce JESUS CHRIST, can't you all see the truth or do you just not want to see the truth? Even some Christians are lost because they are not doing what CHRIST said to do as a Christians. Daniel prophesied the first and the second coming of JESUS CHRIST the MESSIAH in the OLD TESTAMENT, yes the prophetic coming of JESUS CHRIST came hundreds of years before CHRIST was born. GOD had shown Daniel many prophecies. Know the Bible uses day to year format a lot, for example; forty days could be forty years, seven days can be seven years. Also you must remember when the Bible was written, some words may have to be translated from the Greek format. Daniel wanted to know when would these prophecies GOD has shown him come to pass. GOD sent the angel Gabriel to give Daniel his answer. Let's refer to the scripture now.

Daniel 9:24 -25 24 Seventy weeks are determined upon thy people and upon thy holy city, to finish the transgression, and to make an end of sins, and to make reconciliation for iniquity, and to bring in everlasting righteousness, and to seal up the vision and prophecy, and to anoint the MOST HOLY! 25 Know therefore and understand, that the going forth of the commandment to restore and to build Jerusalem unto the MESSIAH the PRINCE shall be seven weeks, and threescore and two weeks: the street shall be built again, and the wall, even in troublous times.

In verse 24 it tells you seventy weeks, and in verse 25 Gabriel tells Daniel exactly when the MESSIAH will come. The scripture says seven weeks and 62 weeks from the time they start rebuilding the temple of Jerusalem which is a total of 69 weeks for the arrival of the MESSIAH. The decree to rebuild the temple of Jerusalem as the book of Ezra records is in 457 B.C. Sixty nine weeks is 483 days. So now when you add the two together we will arrive at when the MESSIAH was on the scene. But now using the day to year format, 483 days is 483 years in this prophecy which brings us to 27 AD (Use the Bible hub chronology site) In 27 AD JESUS calls his first disciples. JESUS is here in the flesh starting his ministry. JESUS came as a man and most expected the MESSIAH to come in his Glory, but JESUS came with the HOLY SPIRIT upon the earth. Now the next time he comes, he will be in his glorious and heavenly attire. Now Angel Gabreil said 70 weeks remember? Where is the other week?

Daniel 9:26 And after threescore and two weeks shall MESSIAH be cut off, but not for himself: and the people of the PRINCE that shall come shall destroy the city and the sanctuary; and the end thereof shall be with a flood, and unto the end of the war desolations are determined.

This prophecy is clearly speaking of the death of the MESSIAH and the crucifixion. Also, notice the scripture says the MESSIAH shall be put to death but not for himself. No because he was put to death for all of us, even the ungrateful who dare not honor his name. The people of the PRINCE which is the Israelites or the Jews will destroy the sanctuary and the city. Now remember this is only a prophecy, but the remarkable part about it is it's an Old Testament prophecy, told hundreds of years BEFORE it happened. WOW! How can any of you deny CHRIST? Let's find out where the other week of the prophecy is.

Daniel 9:27 And He shall confirm the covenant with many for one week: and in the midst of the week he shall cause the sacrifice and the oblation to cease, and for the overspreading of abominations he shall make it desolate, even unto the consummation, and that determined shall be poured upon the desolate.

The MESSIAH shall confirm the covenant with many for ONE WEEK. Thus making week 70 Gabriel confirmed the time the prophecy will happen. You see the way the Jews destroyed their sanctuary and their temple by committing an abomination. When they crucified JESUS on that cross they created an abomination, therefore causing their desolation. CHRIST willfully gave his life, he didn't have to. JESUS' body was the final sacrifice, which put an end to sacrifices and offerings which were written to be done in the middle of the week, But is actually the middle of the 7 yr period he shall cause the sacrifice to cease. What happened in the middle of the seven year period? THE CRUCIFIXION in 30 AD. Remember the day to year format? Let's see it in scripture.

Ezekiel 4:6   And when thou hast accomplished them, lie again on thy right side, and thou shalt bear the iniquity of the house of Judah forty days: I have appointed thee each day for a year.

Always remember, everything you want to need to know is in the Holy Bible. Study and fill yourself with the knowledge and wisdom of the word. Pray for understanding so you will not lean unto your own understanding. I pray this book will guide you and many others to salvation and to Heaven. May GOD bless and have mercy on us all my brothers and sisters in CHRIST. AMEN

L. Patton Christian Author

History is evident. There's only doubt in those who want to doubt. He will come back for the second coming, and I pray we are all ready. In JESUS NAME

AUTHORS BIO

Born in Kansas City, KS in the era of the seventies to teenage parents, it seemed LaDon Patton was dealt a bad hand from birth. She was left to be raised by her grandparents who adopted her. As you can see by her life of testimonies, it's been hard for her, but she was determined to be the victor and not the victim. She went to the United States Army at age 19 in which she served four years and where she also rededicated her life to JESUS CHRIST. She had a son at 18 right before she went to the military, and sought a better life for her and her son. After the military she came home and chose not to reenlist. She went to college and received a certificate for Pharmacy Technician, in which she worked in that field for a while before having a second son. LaDons grandparents raised her but most of her lessons came from life's experiences. Battling outcomes from bad decisions and toxic people, LaDon was only able to find peace in JESUS CHRIST. She said, " It was either give my life to CHRIST or lose my mind." Writing ran in her family, her grandfather was a writer for Reader's Digest and she is a english major. She has a big heart and loves people. She's loyal almost to a fault, and for this reason many people have taken her kindness *for weakness. She said, "it was when I got saved that I learned to deal with people, I pray for them and I only help when the LORD leads me to. Today LaDon is pursuing real estate and becoming a full time writer which is her life's dream. She wrote this book under the instruction of the Holy Spirit. She says, the LORD JESUS CHRIST led her to write this book and she lives her life for CHRIST now and doing well. One thing that's very important to her is that this book reaches many people all over the world.*

GOD BLESS YOU ALL

Isaiah 53:5-6 But he was wounded for our transgressions, he was bruised for our iniquities; the chastisement for our peace was upon him; and with his stripes we are healed. All we like sheep have gone astray; we have turned every one to his own way; and the LORD hath laid on him the iniquity of us all.

In loving memory of my beautiful

mother Mona Lisa Patton

In dedication to my good friend

RIO Nelson

Made in the USA
Monee, IL
13 February 2021